The Star Is Inside

The Star Is Inside

Building a Better Future
Through Youth Sports

Tomás Echeverría

Contents

1

INTRODUCTION

Who is this book for? Who are the expected audiences? Who should read it? And what are the messages that I would like to deliver?

This book is a learning tool for kids and teenagers who play sports, either as amateurs or semiprofessionals. It is an introductory guide about expected behaviors that allow the young ones build life skills that apply in game. These skills will also help them build a stronger foundation for their adult life. Anyone who is directly involved with young athletes will find this book useful, such as parents, coaches, and those participating in sports organizations. All these are the great influencers in children's performance, in their education, in the creation of their values, and in shaping their character and personality traits.

A solid foundation in these soft skills will help children have clarity, strength, and personal virtues from the beginning. This will help, in the future, to build a more viable society as well.

Do you believe that values, such as respect, honesty, discipline, among others, can be cultivated by practicing sports? Do you consider that life skills, such as initiative, teamwork, decision-making, flexibility, and problem-solving, can be developed from an early age? Without a doubt, sports can contribute strongly to the formation of these values and to the construction of these capabilities. Parents and coaches of young players must take care of their growth as human beings, beyond their sports skills.

Focus on values and competencies in sports, beyond the technical and physical skills, is a huge opportunity, and sometimes this opportunity is wasted. Sometimes we put too much pressure on the players, contributing to their frustration, causing them to receive conflicting messages from the coach or from parents. Many kids leave sports at very early ages because they are not having fun. They are not enjoying.

We can achieve outstanding results if we can change the experience of boys and girls during the practice of sports. We can create more awareness and bring a higher consciousness to children's sports. We can do it for the good of our children and future generations of great players and athletes.

2

THE CHALLENGE: MAKING SPORTS A WAY TO JOY

One of my sons at age of fourteen traveled with his soccer team to play a tournament in Spain. They had won three games, and the next day they played a decisive round against the Barcelona team. They were all in the hotel resting, when about seven boys from the team had an act of indiscipline by being absent from their rooms for about two hours, when they were supposed to stay there during rest time. The coach found out what happened but did not know who had been absent from their rooms. During dinner, the coach gathered all the players and asked them who were the players who had left their rooms. Nobody answered. He asked again. Three players out of seven accepted their mistake. The other four players did not answer. The coach punished the three players who told the truth, leaving them out of the game the next day with the Barcelona team. One of those three was my son.

What did they learn? How do we reward kids in sports? What are the values that are most relevant? What kind of message are we giving—telling the truth is being punished and lying allows us to play? How do we educate or train our children beyond penalties for misconduct? How do we teach them to behave better, on and off the field?

Various research[1] and surveys indicate that a child's number one reason for leaving a team sport is the child was not having fun. In this context, we need to ask ourselves some questions: Are our kids enjoying team sports? Are they suffering? Are they receiving too much pressure? Are they developing the behavior that will allow them to thrive in their adult life? Is the practice of sports collaborating in the construction of values and attitudes that will serve your child later in their adult life?

In this sense, ask yourself the following questions: How can I ensure my kids are enjoying the experience? What is the purpose of sports anyway? What values should sports build in our youth? What can I do to ensure that this is happening?

I like to reinforce the importance of enjoying, instead of having fun, playing sports. Joy is the feeling of enjoying what you do. Joy tells that you are doing the right thing, and it is a feeling that stays inside longer. Fun stops when you stop doing what you are doing.

Many kids leave sports at an early age because of the deprivation of joy by parents and coaches. Let me summarize below four key problems that youth sports programs face nowadays, identified by this study and also based on my experience:

a. It focuses only on winning or competing, not enjoying.

The outcome of a game will never be more important than pride of belonging, game experience, friends, and fun.

Those goals are the reasons why many parents, coaches, and volunteers choose to spend time with kids who participate in sports activities. However, somewhere in the process, they forget that enjoying is more important than winning.

After all, only one in six thousand players make it to the NFL, one out of four thousand will make it to the Major League Baseball, and one in ten thousand will reach the NBA, according to the Statistic Brain website. The odds of achieving a child's professional sports dreams are slim, so parents should spend more time helping them enjoy the game.

---

[1]   Researches from The ASPEN Institute Project Play

b. Kids' performance becomes more important than their health.

As the financial costs of youth sports continue to rise, the threat of injury and of not taking proper care of these kids is a much more significant concern. What price are parents willing to pay for their kids to excel in the sports of their choice? Do these kids spend excessive training time depending on their age? How much training is enough?

Many injured athletes continue to play the match because they did not want to leave their coach behind or feared punishment.

We need to be more concerned with a child's life-long health, rather than with their (or their parents') temporary sports aspirations.

c. Kids specialize too young.

Many youth sports programs start with kid's training academies to develop their skills as early as six years old. Very often parents think kids need to have specialized training at early stages, concerned that their kid will lose potential opportunities to play competitive sports or playing colleges.

Many kinds of research show that early sports specialization does not improve the chances of long-term sports success in almost any sport and, otherwise, can increase the risk of injury from excessive practice leading to physical exhaustion.

Circumstances force kids to "specialize" or choose a sport before they are preteens. They dedicate fully to one sport. Rarely do they have the opportunity to experience various sports because coaches expect full attention in the sport; they are playing with them. Commitments to many training sessions per week plus games and money make it almost impossible for kids to play more than one sport. In my personal experience, I appreciate having been able to know and play several sports during my childhood, as I will tell you later.

d. Coaches take more care of the game and results rather than the children.

Some questions parents should ask themselves about their child's sports experience:

- How do I know my child is enjoying the experience?
- Does this game or league serve the needs of kids or the needs of adults? Whose needs are being served?
- What did my child learn from this experience, and does it match the values we are teaching at home? What values do we want our kids to learn?
- Is our family maintaining the order of priorities and values in the education of our kids, or maybe sports are eroding values someway? How can we ensure that sports are reinforcing our values and priorities?

Many kids perceive that conversations with their parents after games are related to a formal evaluation of them. Children may think that their parents valued them based on sports performance and victories or defeats of their team.

Many of us like to cheer on our kids from outside the field. We love to see the feeling of improvement that they feel when we see them playing sports. Let's try to remember why we engaged our kids in youth team sports. It certainly wasn't to be able to become nightmare parents and trainers.

Additionally, most youth coaches do not receive any training in key competencies in working with children. More than four in ten youth coaches say they have never received training in any of the following areas: effective motivational techniques, physical conditioning, or safety needs (general safety/injury prevention and concussion management), according to 2018 data produced for Project Play by the Sports & Fitness Industry Association (SFIA).

Amateur sports games have long been considered vital to a child's healthy development. Adults must ensure that kids are enjoying active participation in youth sports programs. It is, therefore, essential to have a framework that guide them through attributes (see later that we call competencies) needed to emerge stronger from this experience.

As a consequence, one or more relationship begins to break: child-parents, child-coach, parents-coach. When the triangle parent-child-coach breaks in any of the sides, then the child will start to want to quit.

3

MY BACKGROUND

My Player Experience during My Childhood

Since I was a child, I played a lot of sports. I participated in swimming competencies, competitive soccer, tennis, and volleyball teams until I was fifteen years old, when I dedicated only to play tennis. I played the interclub league, and at eighteen, I discovered that my vocation was to teach others to play tennis.

I swam for about four years. I remember an experience in a swimming competition when I was eight years old. It was a freestyle relay 4 x 100 meters race with four swimmers, where I had to start third. I started swimming, and I had to swim 50 meters from the pool and return. The water had a lot of chlorine, and I couldn't see well, and I turned around a few centimeters before without my feet pushing against the wall. When the race ended, the referee approached me to ask me if I had touched the wall on the other side of the pool. My answer was no, and then my team was disqualified. I remember that some teammates and even some parents telling me, "You would have said yes, and we were not disqualified." My father congratulated me for telling the truth, and that was an unforgettable memory of the importance of being honest above sports results.

I was ten years old when I played volleyball, and I remember on weekends we used to go in the coach's van if we played as a visitor. We were twelve children in the van, and the coach gave us the technical talk on the way. The coach was my role model at that time. I wanted to be like him. I imitated his way of speaking, his gestures. When you grow up, you realize how coaches are influential in shaping people's behaviors.

At age of fourteen, I started competing in tennis, playing singles. An individual game like tennis requires a lot of mental strength, something that was not one of my advantages at that age. I was very nervous during games and couldn't bear the pressure during decisive points. I did not enjoy the games because I was nervous, and in that sense, my father decided to withdraw me from the competitions. I would wished at that time I would have had the chance to improve my stress management and problem-solving skills to continue competing.

I have very nice memories of my childhood practicing different sports. All these activities helped me form certain capacities that I later put into practice in my adult life.

My Coaching Experience

At the age of eighteen, I studied for two years to become a tennis coach and worked on that from Monday to Sunday for over eight years. I was fascinated by group classes with many kids. I also taught adults individually or in groups, but my hold to teaching kids and teenagers was what I liked the most.

One of my biggest challenges as a coach was when I had as a player a teenager named Federico, who was partially mentally disabled. He came every morning, two hours a day. After several months of undertaking the tennis lessons, we had plenty of time when we stayed at the bar talking instead of playing tennis.

I remember one day that we couldn't play because it had rained a lot the night before. I decided to take him to a nearby park, and I challenged him to climb a tree. For Federico, it was something completely new that he had never explored before. It was a very motivating new experience for him, away from tennis but very comforting that allowed him to increase his self-confidence after much sacrifice and hard work.

After a while, we started a friendship and then coordinated with his therapist to work on his psychological personality. We began to work on issues of his self-motivation, aspects of his decision-making. We were working on his life skills and personality attributes. Federico's changes after a couple of years were astonishing. Even his tennis performance improved. This experience made me see how much a coach can positively influence the lives of players like Federico, who did not fully enjoy his intelligence like others at his age.

My Corporate Experience

At the age of twenty-four, my corporate career began where I worked for more than twenty-five years with different multinational companies that moved me to live outside Argentina, my native country, living in countries such as Chile, Spain, and the United States. I specialized in managing consultative sales teams for high-value services, primarily in the telecommunications industry.

In the corporate world, it is prevalent to talk about the concept of competencies, as the attributes or abilities that are demonstrated based on expected behaviors. So if the employee behaves in a certain way in a particular trait, he is said to have more or less skill or competence in this regard. Competencies allow, in short, to objectively measure employee behaviors. During part of my professional career, I developed different "competency models" to evaluate the performance of different sales teams.

Throughout my career at Accenture, I have participated in several projects related to defining, managing, and evaluating the skills of professionals in the areas of marketing, sales, and customer service. Additionally, apart from assessing technical knowledge and skills, the expected behaviors were also defined and measured by profile and function at the seniority and level of experience in the position. Also, during my time at Accenture, we wrote a book in 2003 called *eChange - The New Digital Era*, in which I particularly had to write a chapter on "Human Performance." In that chapter, I described all the additional components to the technical knowledge and skills that determine performance; external components such as relationships between people, interpersonal skills, and even aspects such as personal life, family, stress level, economic situation, etc.

During my time at Brightstar, I developed a competency model for the sales force that, on the one hand, allowed me to measure the capabilities of my team at that time. It also helped me develop training plans for those employees who had some competencies to improve. And at the same time, it allowed me to hire new employees measured through this competency model.

I strongly believe that measuring competencies in the field of youth sport has enormous potential and, above all, enormous value for children and teenagers during that critical stage of training for their lives.

My Experience Supporting My Kids Playing Sports

For more than ten years, I participated as the father of the practices, tournaments, and competitive games of my three boys, who play soccer and tennis uninterrupted in the United States. I gathered a lot of good memories and learning experiences playing my role as a father in this youth sports environment.

I remember a bad experience with one of my children, Juan. It was a first practice test to see if Juan liked the soccer club. The practice was over, and all the children were stretching. The coach didn't remember my son's name, so he said, "Hey, you, pretzel, that's not how you do the exercise . . . you look like a pretzel because of the shape of your arms, not like that!" All the children started laughing, and Juan felt very bad. When the practice ended, we got in the car, and he started crying. He told me what had happened. It was a humiliating experience for him. I immediately returned to the place and went to talk to the coach. He naturally replied, "It is very common here to make jokes of children. Do not take it wrong, please." I didn't think it was a convincing answer and decided that my son would continue looking for another club.

I wonder why being a coach gives authority to be tough or rude to children. When we teach our children to walk, are we tough if they fall? When we teach them to eat as babies, do we lose our patience if the food falls from their mouths? Why are we so demanding when we teach sports skills?

Another ugly memory I have was when my eldest son Santiago played soccer and the coach always made funny comments about his technical skills in front of everyone else. He did it sarcastically, near the limit of bulling. Santiago finally quit soccer and started playing tennis.

The sacrifice of parents is very significant if one considers the time spent during the week, time on weekends, trips in and out of state. In many situations, those times are lived with stress, especially during competitions and tournaments. Parents catch this climate of tension. After several years and with my younger children, I began to enjoy watching them play, without being influenced by negative or aggressive comments from parents or coaches.

There is a famous quote from John Sullivan, a former professional soccer player. He said there are only five words we need to tell our kids before, during, and after every game. These five key words are "I love watching you play." That's all, so simple. It's all they need from us, our support, our enjoyment. No judgment, no criticizing. Close your eyes for a moment and imagine the joy of your child while you say these magic words.

My three children played different sports and, in general, had good experiences and great memories they will remember for life. However, they all had some negative experience due to inadequate treatment, excessive pressure, or lack of contention in topics not directly related to sports skills.

That's where I think youth sports organizations need to work a little more; how to take advantage of sport for the formation of values and behaviors of boys that makes them grow more robust and more prepared for their adult life, how to take advantage of sport opportunity to form values and behaviors, how to make youth athletes grow more robust and better prepared for their adult life. I had some conversations with owners of youth sports organizations, and they all agreed there is a big room for improvements beyond teaching just technical and physical skills in sports.

In Summary

In short, throughout my life, I have had to actively participate in three roles that are an essential part of youth sports development. I have been a player, then I have been a coach, and I have been supporting my kids as a father.

In this context, the triangle formed to represent the relationship between the coach, the parents, and the player requires improvement. I consider that sport is a great foundation to educate kids in values, to build character and skills or customs that remain in the young person for the rest of his life. That is the reason why those who surround these kids must align ourselves under a common objective, which has more to do with the building of these competencies or skills that lead them to behave in a certain way, and that will be long-term learning for kids beyond short-term sports results.

In this book, I want to put all my corporate experience and my experience as a player, coach, and father to develop a competency model for youth sport that will allow us to change the culture and focus on building these capacities in our kids. This model will help in ensuring they make a better character, and they grow healthier and more prepared for their future.

4

THE BROKEN TRIANGLE

4.1 Concept

Imagine a triangle with interjoined vertices to the other two vertices through a segment (the side of the triangle). We can represent this triangle as the relationship that is between the coach, the player, and the parents (here, we include mother and father as the same vertex). Each member of the triangle is related to the other two; coach with parents and player, parents with coach and player, and also the player who relates to parents and coach.

These relationships must be guided by the same criteria that we will later call "shared values." In addition to this, each of them must work to improve specific necessary competencies that are vital for their role in this relationship triangle.

The Broken Triangle

4.2   Broken Triangle Situations

I remember countless anecdotes recently lived as a father over the past ten years, and I am sure many of these situations will sound familiar to you.

The stage is a field of play on a game day. On one side of the area, the coach yelling at the players and demanding more effort, discipline, and attitude. The parents are also usually yelling and cheering their children's team across the playing field (sometimes in a wrong manner).

Other times parents were screaming at the players on the opposite side, some parents yelling at the parents of the other groups. These kids respond to provocations from parents and vice versa, reaching the extreme of some parents and coaches, facing expulsion from the referee.

I have seen many coaches screaming throughout the game. Players end up not listening to technical prompts. The player decides to "not listen" to concentrate on the game instead of being aware of the coach's screams.

In a recent publication presented by Victor Carrion, from Stanford University, he describes that children who grow up in environments where screaming is frequent live with high levels of cortisol caused by post-traumatic stress. All this produces a reduction in the size of the hippocampus, a brain structure responsible for processing memories and emotions.

I remember parents, at short distance from the kids, screaming things such as "Come on!" or "Fight for the ball!" or "Pressure, more pressure!" And sometimes even parents are making comments when the team lost the ball or the opponent team score, things like "Oh my god!" or "We cannot lose that ball!" or "Unbelievable!" and many other examples.

Remember also parental verbal abuse of referees and linesmen. This carries over to the boys in disrespect for authority, parents who have to be expelled for insults to the referees, bad experiences for the kids.

How many situations have kids experienced where even with a positive result, they have been criticized by the coach because "they should have left more on the court," and how often the challenge comes because they have lost "for not having followed the coach's instructions"?

How do we think kids take all these screams from both sides of the field during the game? Additionally, they are harangued by the coach when the game ends. The "violence" does not stop here because later, on the way back home, they are harangued by the parents "because they did not do what the father always told him to do" or "because he did not listen to what the coach told him to do." Is it not too much?

I remember a situation when after losing a game, the parents were in the parking lot, getting into the cars. I heard how a father recriminated his son, saying, "I make a lot of financial effort for you to practice this sport. How is it possible that you don't try harder on the field?"

What message are we giving as parents to our children? Do we make them feel guilty? In reality, they are practicing a sport that gives them joy and well-being, isn't it?

Another typical situation is when fathers complain to the coach about the priority given to other kids. Parents have always been the first coaches of their kids in the initiation of a sport. This role of the initial coach must be "transferred" to the official coach who manages the child's growth in games. The father must move to another function, entrusting the authority and sports management of his son to the coach.

There are situations where the relationship between the coach and the players breaks down. I remember for example that one of my sons was in the first team of U13 and the coach established a ranking among the eighteen players of the team based on his opinion about the performance of each player. The coach communicated this ranking to the kids during a practice, reinforcing the idea that the last ones in the ranking had serious risks of downgrading the other team. What message are we giving here to the kids? How do we build a team if the message is that we are competing for a ranking within the same team?

4.3   We Must Strengthen This Triangle

It is our obligation as adults to rebuild this triangular relationship for the good of our kids and youth players who love to develop and grow in their preferred sport. Each component of the triangle must carry out his role in the most efficient way.

Parents need to enjoy watching their kids participate in a sports game. Also, coaches should manage their players with respect and focused on values. Even more important is that kids can be happy about playing sports and increasing their self-esteem.

Coaches need to bet on the education and training of these competencies so that we become aware of the enormous opportunity that sport offers kids and youth players. Some of these opportunities include enabling them to grow sustainably, developing not only technical skills but also soft skills that will allow them to apply later in their life, in other areas beyond sports.

5

FOCUS ON COMPETENCES

5.1 What is a Competency?

The term *competency*, by definition, is the application of knowledge, skills, and behaviors used in performing specific tasks.

The usage of the concept of competency is appropriate in the corporate world, especially in human resources management. Companies use competency models to help their employees grow as professionals and maximize business results.

There is an extensive bibliography that allows companies to manage their human resources and measure their performance based on the definition of competencies that each of the roles or positions of the organization must-have. We can classify skills in different types for various purposes, but I just want to reinforce the main concepts so we can keep the focus on youth sports.

How can we take advantage of all this experience of analysis and management of competencies from the corporate world to the sports world? How can we leverage youth sports education with skills development, such skills that will serve him in the future of his adult life?

In this book, we are going to simplify the concept. We just will focus on competencies, different levels of expertise (proficiency), and expected behaviors based on these levels.

5.2 Competency Levels

Dreyfus[2] brothers created in 1980 a five-stage model that aims to describe the journey of a person from obtaining a skill to mastering it.

5.2.1 Novice

When the individual has little or no experience at all in executing a particular skill; there are plenty of cases to be given as an example, as many people work in the same position for years, ten years of experience on paper, but do not obtain any knowledge nor "experience." The novice aims to succeed and focuses on results rather than education.

5.2.2 Advanced Beginners

The novice evolves by figuring out the mistakes in his work. The newly "promoted" advanced beginner dwells into the world of troubleshooting. Unfortunately, the hasty mindset is not lost, and the individual still aims to acquire results fast, in this case, gain knowledge and information.

5.2.3 Competent

We are in the middle ground of the model. An individual falls into this category when he is fully capable of troubleshooting and solving problems on his own, as well as planning his future actions while avoiding previous mistakes.

5.2.4 Proficient

The individual now looks at the bigger picture. His focus falls onto understanding the essentials of the framework and often experience frustration when documentation is oversimplified. Proficiency, by definition, is the self-improvement skills that each person in the stage has.

---

[2] "A Five-Stage Model of the Mental Activities Involved in Directed Skill Acquisition"

5.2.5 Expert

The fifth and final stage of the model is when the individual becomes an expert in the field. The difference between the fourth and the fifth stage is that people in the fifth are a source of information and knowledge themselves. A significant part of the work done by the expert is intuition-based.

5.3   Behavior Standards

What characteristics must the performance of a person have for them to have developed a specific competence? What are the behaviors expected from a person to determine he is competent?

Behavior standards answer these questions explicitly and accurately. An explicit competency standard describes and exemplifies the level of performance expected in a particular function, collecting the best practices or expected behaviors.

The expected behavior for a particular competency shouldn't be the same as at a novice level or at an expert level. We will see in the coming chapters how we can define expected behaviors for each competency with any degree of proficiency.

These behavior standards are a reference for evaluating and certifying the performance of people based on competencies, and also, it becomes a reference for designing training programs and skills training to develop.

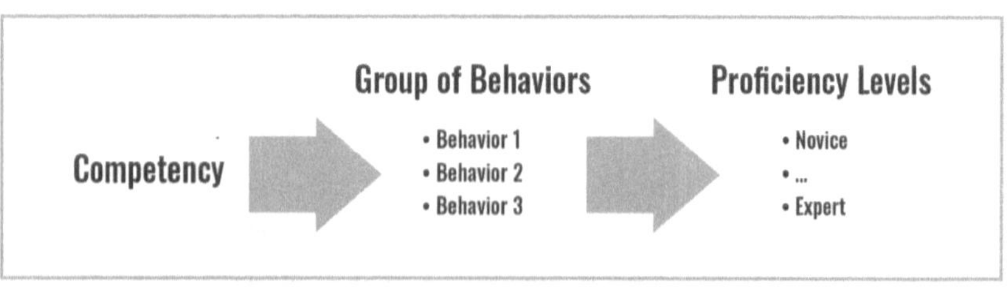

Relationship between Competencies, Expected
Behaviors and Proficiency Levels

COMMITMENT:
"Dedication and commitment are what transforms dreams into realities."

INTEGRITY:
"Integrity is doing the right thing, even when no one is watching."

6

YOUTH SPORT
COMPETENCY MODEL

In the previous chapter, we have developed the concept of competencies, what they mean, what they are for, and how to put them to practical use, where their benefits are measurable over time. Now we focus on building the youth sports competency model.

6.1   Components of the Model.

The objective of the competency model is to have a framework that allows us to measure and maximize the performance, in this case, of kids practicing a youth sport.

In this context, many components affect the performance of an athlete, what I define the AVC (abilities, values, competencies) components, among which we find

- **A**bilities related to the sport:
  - o   Technical
  - o   Physical
  - o   Mental
- **V**alues (beliefs)

- **C**ompetencies (behavior)

In the youth sports competency model that we will focus on in this book, we will remove from the analysis of the abilities directly related to the sport, that is, the technical, physical, and mental skills of the player. Can we assume that two kids with similar sports abilities can have different results and obtain various performances in different ways? Absolutely.

Surely, they have met a child or adolescent who has excellent technical ability, a lot of skill and physical coordination, but whose attitudes and behaviors at the time of the competition are not adequate. Even on many occasions, I have seen how these "attitudinal overflows" or anti-disciplinary practices are "accepted" because he is the most skillful of the team. Are we tolerating or accepting lousy behavior just by prioritizing game technique?

The "soft" skills or competencies that determine behaviors and the values or beliefs that define the convictions of the different participants in the relationship triangle undoubtedly determine the high-performance performance that a player can achieve. It not only determines the results in the short-term sport, but more importantly, it also determines the construction of skills that will be used in the future life of the player when he is an adult. Building these soft skills allows coaches, parents, and kids to look at life differently and put sport as a powerful life-learning tool.

6.2 Applying AVC in Youth Sport

I'm pretty sure that all or most youth sports organizations are playing a significant role in coaching kids and youth sports players in their abilities to play the sport they love. These abilities include detailed technical preparation, physical training, and some coaching regarding mental skills, especially before and after the game.

Most youth sports organizations also have their values defined. Those values are communicated through their web sites and banners across the fields, although sometimes these values are not followed by coaches and community members, such as parents and kids.

However, when we talk about expected behavior, there is not like a common standard about what is required to succeed. Maybe *success* is not the right word since kids and youth sports players improving their competency levels will gain something valuable for their entire life. Are the youth sports organizations contributing to this growth? (How are youth sports organizations contributing to this growth?) There is a huge opportunity out there to leverage these daily interactions with kids to leverage these concepts and to build better human beings for the future.

6.3   The Framework of Youth Sport Competency Model

Below is a description of the framework of the youth sports competency model, where, on the one hand, we leave out the detailed analysis of the technical skills, physical abilities, and technical knowledge of the game. They are part of the model because an athlete must ultimately have that knowledge and skills, but they are not part of the central message of this book. Instead, we focus on highlighting the competencies of the coach, the player, and the parents that surround the player.

We see that there are competencies that are common to the three roles and that each role also has specific skills to develop to interact well with the other characters and maximize team performance.

As a central axis, the three roles must naturally share, live, and breathe the core values on which the relationship must focus. The common core values are the spirit of teamwork between the coach, the player, and the parents.

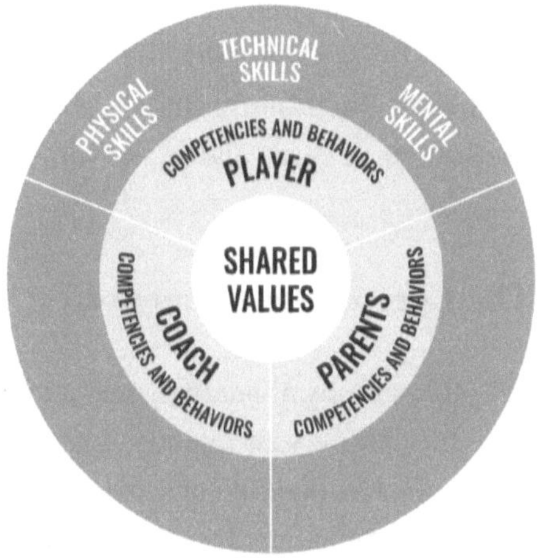

Youth Sport Competency Framework

6.3.1 Abilities Are Out of the Analysis

As described earlier, abilities are those skills required or directly related to the sport.

- Technical abilities refer to specific procedures to move one's body to act. Examples of technical skills are dribbling, passing, shooting, serving, smashing, pivoting, others.
- Physical abilities generally focus on developing motor skills, such as strength, power, endurance, speed, coordination, agility, balance.
- You may hear sports coaches often say that games are 80 percent mental and 20 percent physical. That's true. Training your mind is as essential as preparing your body and technique.

These skills are valid for sports, especially when it comes to highly competitive games. But how many children who play sports become professionals? How many children do sports receive a scholarship to play at the university? How do we help the vast majority who do not dedicate their lives to a competitive game develop as people?

The purpose of this book is to build competencies[3] that will allow young people to be more successful in their adult life. Such skills include their interaction with other people, their future studies, their work relationships, their relationships with their partner, and in the future education of their children.

6.3.2 Values: The Core of the Framework

There is so much bibliography about the value and why living through values is essential for life. Many youth sports organizations define their importance; however, sometimes these values are not followed or monitored over time, ensuring their prioritization. I would consider that there are five values to be shared between players, coaches, and parents. In my opinion, these values represent the pillar of relationships, and these five values are the base of everything.

1. **Integrity** means doing the right thing in the right way; it means adhering to values firmly held. Operating with integrity fosters mutual goodwill and support, which leads to an improved sense of team spirit, mutual loyalty, and team resilience. I would say there is a secure connection between integrity in sports and sportsmanship, defined as ethical, appropriate, polite, and fair behavior while participating in a sports game.

2. **Commitment** is one of the values that underpin strong and mutually beneficial relationships. People who can maintain stable relationships rank high in their emotional intelligence, and they are the most likely to fulfill their commitments or stay committed. It is so because it takes emotional competence to sacrifice time, to exercise considerable will, and to exert substantial effort. It is the attitude of sincere and dedicated focus on purpose.

3. **Discipline.** One of the essential things in life is learning to train yourself to know your limits and goals. Not only in sport, but also in life, having discipline helps you achieve success, better and

---

[3] "Harvard Competency Dictionary", "The Nielsen Group Soft Skills", "Society for Human Resource Management Competency Model", and many others

faster. It also teaches you that not everything will be a victory and that next time, you must work harder.

4. **Respect:** Having respect for their coaches in sport helps kids later in life when it comes to adults or authority figures. Understanding that you don't know everything at a young age may help you in the future when you speak or listen to people older and wiser than you.

5. **Joy** is what keeps kids coming back to play. Kids should be enjoying in sports. This value should be shared and prioritized with coaches and parents. Joy and dedication can play in the same field. Joy should both be part of the youth sports experience. If the team has joy in the process of being challenged, they will learn to love the game.

6.3.3 Competencies for Youth Sports Players

Below is a list of the main competencies that young athletes can develop while playing sports:

1. **Communication.** Conveying information and ideas to individuals or groups in a manner that engages the audience and helps them understand and retain the message.

2. **Teamwork.** Contributing to the team's success, actively participating as a team member to help you achieve your goals.

3. **Problem-Solving.** Identifying alternative solutions to a problem and selecting the best option, identifying the system component that is causing the error as well as the options available for resolving it and completing the tasks.

4. **Leadership.** Organizing and motivating people to get things accomplished in a way that everyone feels a sense of order and direction.

5. **Accountability.** Taking responsibility for all work activities and personal actions, following through on commitments, implementing decisions that others agree upon, maintaining confidentiality with sensitive information, acknowledging and learning from mistakes without blaming others.

6. **Self-Motivation.** Doing what needs to be done without influence from other people or situations. Players with self-motivation can find a reason and strength to complete a task, even when challenging, without giving up or needing another to encourage them.
7. **Decision-Making.** Identifying and understanding problems and opportunities using practical approaches to choose a course of action during practice and competition, taking action consistent with available facts and limitations.
8. **Stress Management.** Maintaining stable performance under pressure or opposition (such as time pressure or job ambiguity), managing stress in a way that is acceptable to others and the organization.
9. **Adaptability.** Maintaining effectiveness even when experiencing significant changes in training or competition environment; adjusting to playing within new structures, processes, requirements, or cultures.
10. **Attention to Detail.** Seeing and paying attention to details, recognizing parts of a procedure or object, and verifying the correctness or error in an individual piece or process.
11. **Persistence.** Staying the course in times of difficulty, remaining motivated to accomplish goals in the face of adversity or obstacles.
12. **Initiative.** Taking quick steps to achieve your goals; taking steps to achieve goals beyond what is required; being proactive
13. **Applied Learning.** Assimilating and applying coach-related information promptly.
14. **Continuous Learning.** Actively identifying new areas for learning, regularly creating and taking advantage of learning opportunities, using newly acquired knowledge and skills
15. **Risk-Taking.** Initiating action that tries to achieve a recognized benefit or advantage when potential negative consequences are understood.

6.3.4 Competencies for a Sports Coach

In the same sense, coaches can develop other human competencies more related to their role and that go beyond their technical and sports knowledge:

1. **Building a Successful Team.** Using appropriate methods and a flexible interpersonal style to help build a cohesive team, facilitating the fulfillment of the team's goals. The main goal for coaches should be making the players learn to have joy and sustain it.
2. **Building Trust.** Interacting with others in a way that gives them confidence in one's intentions and those of the organization.
3. **Coaching.** Providing timely guidance and feedback to help others strengthen specific skill areas necessary to accomplish a task or solve a problem.
4. **Developing Others.** Planning and supporting the development of the abilities and skills of individuals so that they can fulfill current or future responsibilities more effectively.
5. **Managing Conflict.** Dealing effectively with others in an antagonistic situation, using appropriate interpersonal styles and methods to reduce tension or conflict between two or more people.
6. **Planification and Organization.** Establishing courses of action for oneself and others, ensuring efficient completion of work, managing time and resources to ensure the practical end of practice.
7. **Work Standards.** Setting high-performance standards for yourself and others, taking responsibility and accountability for completing self-imposed tasks or measures of excellence rather than having imposed standards, identifying and correcting conditions that affect a player's safety.
8. **Communication.** Transmitting information and ideas to individual players or groups in a way that engages the audience and helps them understand and retain the message.

9. **Leadership.** Organizing and motivating people to get things accomplished in a way that everyone feels a sense of order and direction.

10. **Valuing diversity.** Appreciating and taking advantage of the capacities and ideas of all members of the team, working with individuals of diverse styles, abilities, and motivations.

6.3.5 Competencies for Parents

Finally, parents, who must also work internally to develop these skills that will allow their child to practice sport with greater joy and enthusiasm:

1. **Acceptance.** Accepting your child as he/she is, with his/her limitations, wishes, and capabilities; understand his/her dreams; respecting his/her decisions.

2. **Delegation.** Assigning of decision-making authority and responsibility for the task to appropriate others to maximize the effectiveness of the team and individuals.

3. **Adaptability.** Maintaining effectiveness even when experiencing significant changes in training or competition environment, adjusting to playing within new structures, processes, requirements, or cultures.

4. **Building Trust.** Interacting with others in a way that gives them confidence in one's intentions and those of the organization.

5. **Communication.** Conveying information and ideas to individuals or groups in a manner that engages the audience and helps them understand and retain the message.

6. **Developing Others.** Planning and supporting the development of the abilities and skills of individuals so that they can fulfill current or future responsibilities more effectively.

7. **Listening.** Hearing what your kids say without judgment.

6.4 Summary of Core Values and Competencies by Role

There is a sharing of many competencies between different roles; however, the expected behavior by function is not the same.

Shared Core Values	
1. Integrity	4. Respect
2. Commitment	5. Joy
3. Discipline	

Player Competencies	Coach Competencies	Parents Competencies
1. Communication	1. Building a Team	1. Acceptance
2. Teamwork	2. Building Trust	2. Delegation
3. Problem-Solving	3. Coaching	3. Adaptability
4. Leadership	4. Developing Others	4. Building Trust
5. Accountability	5. Managing Conflict	5. Communication
6. Self-Motivation	6. Planning and Organizing	6. Developing Others
7. Decision Making	7. Work Standards	7. Listening
8. Stress Management	8. Communication	
9. Adaptability	9. Leadership	
10. Attention to Details	10. Valuing Diversity	
11. Persistence		
12. Initiative		
13. Applied Learning		
14. Risk-Taking		

The expected behaviors for each of these competencies and their way of measuring are analyzed in the following chapters.

RESPECT:
"Respect should be the first thing you give."

TEAMWORK:
"Teamwork divides the tasks and multiplies the success."

7

MEASURING YOUR COMPETENCIES

7.1 Importance of Measuring Competencies

Competency assessment, by definition, is any process for measuring and documenting player competency. The goal of competency assessment is to identify problems with the player performance and to correct these issues before they affect performance.

Competency assessment provides a benchmark for performance management and player development. An initial competency assessment may reveal the need for specific training or improvement opportunities.

7.2 How Does it Work?

The graph below describes the group of expected behaviors for each competency and the rating for the competency level (novice to expert). For each skill and each associated behavior level indicator, there is a rating linked to the competencies.

Competency Assessment Matrix for Players

Competency	Group of Expected Behaviors	(1)	(2)	(3)	(4)	(5)
Communication	• Asks clear questions • Receives instructions, orders, or assignments • Clearly communicates ideas in a group setting • Receptive to ideas or suggestions from others • Uses appropriate nonverbal communication (eye contact, gestures, posture) when communicating with others					
Teamwork	• Collaborates with others to accomplish tasks, assignments, etc. • Supports group decisions, even if not in total agreement • Shares credit for good ideas or accomplishments with peers, team members, and others • Cooperatively trains with peers, team members, and others to set responsibilities (e.g., agree on schedules or rotations) • Asks for input from peers, team members, and others • Shares information, ideas, and solicit ideas and suggestions from others to accomplish mutual goals					
Problem-Solving	• Accurately assesses the situation and arrives at a positive solution • Deals with playing time issues • Learns ways to balance schedules between school and sports					
Leadership	• Builds relationships with teammates, peers, and players • Embodies the positive side of passion • Infuses this in the minds of fellow players • Motivates other players to be better every day					
Accountability	• Shows up to practice on time and follows instructions, policies, and procedures • Stays focused on tasks despite distractions and interruptions • Makes the best use of available time and resources • Does not make excuses for errors or problems, acknowledges and corrects mistakes • Accepts personal responsibility for quality, achieves results with little oversight					

Self-Motivation	• Looks on the bright side, thinks positively • Shows ability to "bounce back" after a setback, keeps positivity in the face of challenges • Believes in one's potential to improve • Visualizes oneself in the wished situation and enjoys						
Decision Making	• Quickly makes decisions during tough situations • Anticipates the consequences of decisions • Creates appropriate options for addressing problems/opportunities and achieves desired outcomes • Takes action or generate alternative solutions to resolve problems						
Stress Management	• Deals with unclear situations • Accordingly copes with conflicting training demands • Handles distractions or interruptions • Deals with rush situations (one thing at a time, flow, not rush) • Remains flexible, open, and decisive in the face of changing needs						
Adaptability	• Treats change and new situations as opportunities for learning or growth • Focuses on the beneficial aspects of change • Quickly modifies one's behavior to deal with changes in the environment • Does not persist with ineffective behaviors						
Attention to Details	• Accurately and carefully follows established procedures for completing tasks • Ensures that all details of a task are accomplishable • Keeps track of many small details without forgetting any • Is being watchful over a while						
Persistence	• Focuses to achieve a goal despite barriers or difficulties, focuses to overcome obstacles by changing strategies, doubling efforts, using multiple approaches, etc. • Adjusts focus when it becomes evident that a goal cannot be achieved, redirects energy into related achievable goals when appropriate						

Initiative	• Volunteers for task force assignments that are beyond the normal limits of the job • Identifies ways to make a job more comfortable or more productive • Collects extra information that might be useful for others • Volunteers to help peers • Suggests ways to solve problems, etc., without being asked					
Applied Learning	• Actively participates in learning activities • Readily absorbs and comprehends new information from formal and informal learning experiences • Puts new knowledge, understanding, or skill to practical use					
Risk-Taking	• Makes decisions when the probability of success is unclear • Makes decisions that involve risk • Tries new but unproven approaches to solving problems					

(1) Novice,   (2) Advanced Beginner,   (3) Competent,   (4) Proficient,   (5) Expert

Competency Assessment Matrix for Coaches

Competency	Group of Expected Behaviors	(1)	(2)	(3)	(4)	(5)
Building a Team	• Communicates the purpose and importance of the team through a clear charter or mission statement • Sets specific and measurable team goals and objectives • Values and uses individual differences and talents to ensure that the team works • Focuses on enjoying the game and or practice and the lessons learned • Regularly shares information with the team • Does not badly speak of the team to others					
Building Trust	• Strictly follows the organization's policies • Appropriately handles confidential personnel records and does not share confidential information • Fairly and equally treats individuals • Maintains an open-door policy and listens to others' comments, suggestions, and complaints • Keeps promises and commitments • Shows genuine interest in the success of others and promote and showcase their abilities					
Coaching	• Instructs players and carefully guides their activities • Helps each player define his/her individual goals • Works with players to strengthen their performance and improve their skills in a particular area to achieve their individual goals • Teaches players how to successfully complete new tasks/procedures • Determines how much guidance an individual need to successfully complete a task • Listens to players' concerns about their ability to improve • Provides feedback about performance on a task or activity that is specific and objective • Reinforces others' successful performance • Diagnoses problems and shares solutions to create learning experiences • Demonstrates practical problem-solving approaches					

Developing Others	• Involves players in determining developmental goals and actions • Helps and encourages players to determine and develop the skills necessary for current and future jobs • Considers players' motivations, interests, and current situations in planning long-range developmental activities • Designs or locates appropriate training programs for players					
Managing Conflict	• Settles disputes between players • Settles disputes between groups within the organization • Settles disputes as quickly as possible • Watches for conflicts to prevent them from growing • Keeps relationships smooth even during stressful times • Educates players on how to deal with conflict					
Planning, Organizing	• Plans use of own time to accomplish a variety of tasks • Schedules your work so that the most important work gets done • Prepares plans for medium-term (including tasks, resources, and time frames) • Develops timetables or milestone charts for projects					
Work Standards	• Sets high standards of work performance for self • Sets high standards of performance for the team, group, or others • Reviews others' work for quality • Provides encouragement and support to others in accepting responsibility					
Communication	• Asks clear questions • Provides instructions, orders, or assignments • Clearly communicates ideas in a group setting • Receptive to ideas or suggestions from others • Uses appropriate nonverbal communication (eye contact, gestures, posture) when communicating with others					

| Leadership | • Creates a positive environment where all team members are motivated to do their best by ensuring each participant knows his goals and understands how he can achieve them
• Builds confidence in a group's ability to address challenges
• Links mission, vision, values, goals, and strategies to everyday activities
• Sees the potential in others and takes opportunities to apply and develop that potential
• Takes calculated risks or tries a fresh approach to improve performance or reach a challenging goal
• Sets clear, meaningful, challenging, and attainable group goals and expectations that align with those of the organization
• Suggests and asks for others' ideas to improve quality, efficiency, and effectiveness | | | | | |
| Valuing Diversity | • Participates in local diversity efforts
• Supports local diversity efforts
• Takes action or seeks appropriate resources when issues arise | | | | | |

(1) Novice,   (2) Advanced Beginner,   (3) Competent,   (4) Proficient,   (5) Expert

Competency Assessment Matrix for Parents

Competency	Group of Expected Behaviors	(1)	(2)	(3)	(4)	(5)
Acceptance	• Accepts one's child as he/she is, accepts his/her limitations, wishes, and capabilities. • Understands his/her dreams • Respects his/her decisions					
Delegation	• Respects the delegated areas of decision-making • Respects coach's decisions					
Adaptability	• Views change and new situations as opportunities for learning or growth • Focuses on the beneficial aspects of change • Quickly modifies one's behavior to deal with changes in the environment • Readily tries new approaches appropriate for new or changed situations • Does not persist with ineffective behaviors					

Building Trust	<ul><li>Strictly follows the organization's policies</li><li>Appropriately handles confidential personnel records and does not share confidential information</li><li>Fairly and equally treats individuals</li><li>Maintains an open-door policy and listens to others' comments, suggestions, and complaints</li><li>Keeps promises and commitments</li><li>Shows genuine interest in the success of others and promotes and showcases their abilities</li></ul>					
Communication	<ul><li>Clearly communicates ideas in a group setting</li><li>Receptive to ideas or suggestions from others</li><li>Uses appropriate nonverbal communication (eye contact, gestures, posture) when communicating with others</li></ul>					
Developing Others	<ul><li>Involves their children in determining developmental goals and actions</li><li>Helps and encourages players to determine and develop the skills necessary for current and future jobs</li><li>Considers players' motivations, interests, and current situations in planning long-range developmental activities</li><li>Designs or locates appropriate training programs for players</li></ul>					

(1) Novice,　　(2) Advanced Beginner,　　(3) Competent,　　(4) Proficient,　　(5) Expert

Also, the assessment related to core values can be measured:

Shared Values	Group of Expected Behaviors	(1)	(2)	(3)	(4)	(5)
Integrity	<ul><li>Keeps your promises even if it takes extra effort</li><li>Does not gossip or badly talk about someone</li><li>Does not let someone else take the blame for something one did</li><li>Does not tell anyone what you know, if someone gives you confidential information.</li></ul>					

		(1)	(2)	(3)	(4)	(5)
Commitment	• Has a detailed plan on how to achieve their goals • Focuses on the process more than results • Maintains good habits (healthy nutrition, sleeps at a decent hour, makes a recovery after practice, among others) • Is a student of your sport • Stays positive and motivated when struggling					
Discipline	• Learns to sacrifice some things • Learns to deal with losses to improve performance next time • Learns how to set and accomplish goals • Learns the value of practice and preparation					
Respect	• Respect yourself, respect your own emotions, and your own needs. • Respects your opponent. There is no place for harassing comments, gamesmanship, or other actions that might humiliate the other side. • Respects the officials. If there's a questionable call during a game, athletes should quietly and appropriately ask for an explanation. • Respects the game. Anything that is not about playing the game or communicating with teammates can lead to disrespect for the sport. • Respects your resources. Demonstrate respect for facilities and equipment.					
Joy	• Believes that enjoyment is the primary reason for playing sports • Seeks pleasure from participation • Provides emotional support and positive feedback					

(1) Novice,   (2) Advanced Beginner,   (3) Competent,   (4) Proficient,   (5) Expert

7.3 Type of Assessments

Just as an illustration, I propose carrying out cross-assessment, where each one evaluates himself in his role, and meetings can also be held for the evaluation of skills and feedback. All communication in this sense is always beneficial for each of the participating roles.

7.3.1 Self-Assessment

While not to be used alone, self-assessments are an excellent method for providing individuals with the opportunity to rate themselves against a measurable competency model. Self-assessments allow players, coaches, and parents to reflect on their strengths and weaknesses while getting a sense of the areas in which they need further development.

It is important to note that self-assessments used on their own cannot provide accurate assessments. This is caused by individual bias, where one will either rate himself or herself below or above the competency level.

7.3.2 Coach Assessment (top-down)

The coach can only conduct an assessment after having ample time to monitor and assess the player.

An excellent way to do this is to provide the player with assignments and tasks that test the competencies. Similar to how individuals bias self-assessments, it is crucial for coaches to be aware of their preferences to be as objective as possible.

7.3.3 360-Degree Assessment (bottom-up)

The most accurate results are from 360-degree assessments. Individuals are rated as objectively as possible from every conceivable angle. Because of this, 360-degree assessments are one of the most popular and widely-accepted methods for measuring competencies. To complete a 360-degree evaluation, begin by getting the individual to rate themselves through a self-assessment.

7.4 Assessment Realization

Now is time to combine all the previous concepts into the assessment execution. We have the competences, we have the maturity levels, and we have the templates for the assessments. So who should assess who? Again, this is a proposal, but each sports organization can take its own methodology and adapt it to its needs.

Who Should Assess Who?

Player	Coach	Parents
1. Self-Assessment 2. 360-assess to Coach	3. Self-Assessment 4. Player assessment	5. Self-Assessment 6. 360-assess to Coach

- Meeting A needs to happen between Player and Coach to review:
  - o Player Self-Assessment (1) against Manager to Player assessment (4)
- Meeting B needs to happen after Meeting A between Coach and Parents to review:
  - o Achieving A results between Coach and Player
  - o Coach Self-Assessment (3) and 360-assessment to Coach (6)
- Parents need to evaluate outcomes after Meetings A and B and review internally their self-assessment

It is very common in all youth sports organizations that there are periodic meetings between the coach, the player, and the parents to make a technical evaluation of the child. This is an excellent opportunity to introduce the concept of competencies and to start measuring and evaluating improvement in these aspects as well.

I wonder how a coach handles the ego of a player who is very skilled, perhaps the best on his team. I wonder also how parents can let the coach know the main personal characteristics of their child (beyond their sports skills) where sport can help them develop their weakest competences. Fostering not only sports skills but also developing competences puts the club on another level. It is a differentiator factor.

Ultimately, this model creates value for all stakeholders, and it is a win-win situation for both clubs, coaches and parents, delivering all these benefits to the players.

ACCOUNTABILITY:
"Accountability: The glue that ties commitment to results."

INITIATIVE:
"Don't wait for the perfect moment. Take the
moment and make it perfect."

8

DESIGNING A COMPETENCY DEVELOPMENT PROGRAM

Competency-based training is one of the most critical pieces of a competency development program, so let's review the central concept of competency-based training:

8.1 Competency-Based Training

Competency-based training is an approach to designing learning programs with a focus on competencies (knowledge, skills, and abilities) rather than time spent in a classroom. Competency-based education combines an intentional and transparent approach to curricular design with an academic model, in which the time it takes to demonstrate competencies varies, and the expectations about learning are held constant.

Students acquire and demonstrate their knowledge and skills by engaging in learning exercises, activities, and experiences that align with clearly-defined programmatic outcomes. Students receive proactive guidance and support from faculty and staff. Learners earn credentials by demonstrating mastery through multiple forms of assessment, often at a personalized pace.

Competency-based training differs from other non-related approaches in that the unit of learning is extremely fine-grained.

- Rather than a course or a module, every individual skill or learning outcome (known as a competency) is one single unit.
- Players, coaches, and parents work on one competency at a time, which is likely a small component of a larger learning goal.
- The student is evaluated on the individual competency and can only move on to other competencies after they have mastered the current skill they are learning.
- After that, higher or more complex competencies are learned to a degree of mastery and are isolated from other topics.

8.2 Traditional Approach - Program Stages

8.2.1 Planning

Before starting a competency-based training program, it's important to lay some groundwork and create a master plan for your approach. In the planning stages, decision-makers within your organization need to agree on your core competencies. It is vital to make your intentions clear to everyone in the organization and, if possible, provide an outline with goals, deadlines, and expectations.

8.2.2 Give Assessments

You can begin to give assessments to find out where the players stand competency-wise. While evaluations are a vital part of the discovery process, for many (including the team member under evaluation), the term "assessment" carries a lot of negative baggage. A couple of different types of assessments include self-assessments, coach assessments, 360 assessment, or a combination of all these. It's essential to make sure the players understand the purpose of the evaluation.

8.2.3 Create a Framework for Competency-Based Learning

After the planning and assessments stages are complete, it's time to create a competency-based training framework. Together with all levels of management, it's essential to lay out a plan that will work for your organization. Make sure to develop a training framework aligned with your competency development goals.

When creating a framework for competency-based training, keep in mind:

- Ease of use – If the program is hard to understand, students can get frustrated.
- Motivation – If students can't see the goal or don't understand how the program is benefiting them, they won't push themselves to meet your goals.

8.2.4 Align Competency-Based Learning with Assessments

To make the most out of your training, use the data gathered from your assessments to decide where the skill gaps exist. Convey this information to management and decide on the skill areas you want to develop. Prioritize these skill gaps and develop a plan, set deadlines, and empower your staff throughout this process. Teams and players must understand the goal, or they won't feel motivated. Explain to staff that by building their skill sets and expanding their competencies, they'll be benefiting personally from this process in addition to helping the club as a whole.

8.2.5 Implement Competency-Based Learning

What makes competency-based training programs stand out against more generic training is that they specifically target the skills needed to expand and improve an organization's core competencies. Along with an overall competency development plan, this provides the best return on investment for the youth sport organization.

There are several ways to implement competency-based training programs, including, but not limited to, one-on-one training sessions, workshops, e-courses, individual and self-paced, in a group setting with an instructor, and more. Remember that when people, in general, starts a training program, there are these two things to consider:

1. Each individual comes with varying levels of knowledge about the subject.
2. Each individual has different learning styles as well as all the other non-work-related things happening in their lives. They are going to learn at different paces.

No matter what format you decide upon, make sure that your learning program is conducive to those who are taking the courses.

8.2.6 Make Use of Competency-Based Learning Management Software

To provide staff with the best learning experience possible, as well as create a framework that is sustainable and will be usable for years to come, implementing competency-based learning management system software (LMS) is crucial. Providing staff with an e-learning option allows for a customized, self-paced learning experience: a structure that makes sense for all involved.

The LMS should include the ability to track all learning activities of your employees, define and track employee certifications, and customize the LMS to meet your workforce's specific needs. By implementing learning management system software, data is easily accessible by coaches and top management. This system allows for quick and easy decision-making and ongoing skills gap analysis.

8.2.7 Analyze and Revise

After the implementation of your competency-based training program, it's essential to continue to improve upon the framework—collect data, interview staff, speak with management, and make changes to your training program based on your findings. This practice will create the most sustainable competency-based training program going forward.

8.3   The Challenge of Engagement

The traditional approach of competency-based training summarizes all the steps necessary to measure and develop new behaviors, building those human capacities and soft skills. However, many times this approach is not effective since it does not generate great engagement in organizations.

If we think about children between eight and fifteen years old, it would be very difficult to achieve this engagement with the traditional approach. That is why the new trend for both adults, but especially for children, is to focus on learning these skills through play.

In this sense, the concept of game-based learning, I think, is more applicable for children. Game-based learning is a branch of serious games that deals with applications that have defined learning outcomes. Generally, they are designed in order to balance the subject matter with the gameplay and the ability of the player to retain and apply said subject matter to the real world.

So basically, game-based learning is nothing more than a genre of serious games specifically for learning purposes. Playing a game is an activity of improving skills in order to overcome these challenges, and playing a game is, therefore, fundamentally a learning experience. Games offer a situated practice, where we as players must acquire the skills, knowledge, and competencies needed to beat the game.

A recent research called "Game-Based Learning Contexts for Soft Skills,"[4] developed in 2017, describes the results of the use of game-based learning with the goal to improve soft skills. The main skills developed were leadership, organization, decision-making, resources management, financial skills, team management, time management, and managing stress.

---

[4]   Sousa, Maria & Rocha, Álvaro. (2017). Game Based Learning Contexts for Soft Skills

DECISION-MAKING:
"Every accomplishment began with a decision to try."

ADAPTABILITY:
"When we are no longer able to change a situation,
we are challenged to change ourselves."

9

WHAT DOES SUCCESS MEAN?

How do you know the athletes have improved? How can you measure and ensure sport delivers expected results in athletes during a medium- to long-term period?

Once the coach has developed the framework and measured the behaviors, he can assess the progress of the participant and determine the grade of evolution. When can we consider the program has been successful?

Many relevant definitions of success come to my mind:

Dalai Lama says that "being successful in life means that the individual carries a meaningful life." Henry Thoreau, an American philosopher, said, "If you advance confidently in the direction of your dreams and endeavor to live the life which you have imagined you will meet with a success unexpected in common hours." Finally, the definition that I like the most is the one made by the author Wayne Dyer. He said, "Success is an inner process; it is something you bring to everything you do in your life."

In my opinion, success is not a result in itself but rather an internal state. In the context of youth sports, I would speak of a state of internal joy rather than a state of success. How many times does it happen to us in sports that we do not achieve the common goal (win the game or the tournament) but the team feels that its performance has improved and the state of happiness is immense? Similarly, we may have had a good result and were not happy with the performance.

What is meaningful to one participant could be meaningless to another. One child might want to participate in sports to have more friends or long-lasting friendships, while another could want to develop self-trust. These goals are personal and different for each person. It is important to identify these goals from the beginning to offer the participant an adequate program for his/her development. Also, by pursuing these inner goals, the participants will feel that their journey has a meaning and every step of the way they will feel that they are succeeding.

In the context of amateur sports, especially youth and children's sports, the result should not determine the mood of the players, coaches, or parents.

The old paradigm considers the idea that if someone wins, then the other loses. The games and the competition have a result, but you can always win, both teams can win, and that is a value that we must give to our children.

In the new paradigm, we are all one, and we measure success individually, against our individual goals. What is success for one person may not be success for another one.

It is important to focus on the journey, enjoying the training sessions, enjoying the interaction with colleagues, enjoying the construction of these competencies or soft skills without focusing so much on the final results these competencies may bring over the years, but focusing instead on a daily state of the soul that should be state of joy and fun for the children and teenagers.

I remember that one of my sons had a coach who did not focus on results but defined a goal for each game that had to do with learning a tactical play. In the first games of the season, the team lost, 4-0, but nevertheless, the coach was happy. The coach's message to his players at the end of the game had to do with the application of the technical tactics or skills that he had defined as objectives in that game. "I'm happy because we had four corners that we kicked with our left leg directly to the near post and the forwards coordinated very well," that was today's goal.

"But we lost, 4-0," some parents said.

"It does not matter," said the coach. "The important thing is the construction of skills. The results will come as a result of this work."

This is what I mean by enjoying the journey, being aware of the learning process, and this applies to the construction of technical, physical, mental, and also life skills or behaviors.

To achieve a state of joy is as important as to continue to be in a state of joy. We should encourage athletes to maintain this internal state of joy continuously over time while competencies or life skills are being developed. This concept also applies to technical or physical skills directly related to the sport we practice. We should facilitate athletes to focus on the journey of mastering skills instead of performing and comparing themselves with others. This comparison only makes them compete between one another. Comparing themself causes anxiety, dissatisfaction, and takes the athletes away from that state of joy. This is the old paradigm, and we should avoid the "us versus them" approach.

Children will reach a state of joy as soon as they find a meaning to what they do, that is, as soon as they feel that what they are doing allows them to fulfill their wishes. To sustain this, it will require a long-term plan of development that adequately support his/her inner goals and a thorough monitoring of the plan. This is described in detail in Chapter 7 – Measuring Your Competences.

We are used to focusing on the results. It is part of what we have learned since we were children. We want results. We want to measure whether we have reached the desired goals. Outcome is everything. We want to be successful.

I'm not saying it's not important. It is important to define objectives and working hard in order to achieve those proposed goals. However, my vision is that only focusing on results makes us more unhappy. If we only focus on results, the only thing we will do is compare ourselves with who did it better than us.

STRESS MANAGEMENT:

"The greatest weapon against stress is our ability to choose one thought over another."

PERSISTENCE:

"The only place that success comes before work is in the dictionary."

10

RECOMMENDATIONS

Finally, I would like to review what central concepts we saw in this book. We all understand that children should be happier playing sports and that many times, for different reasons, they suffer a lot of frustration and receive bad habits or old beliefs, both from parents and coaches. We need to change this.

We review that broken triangle that occurs between the player and the coach, between the coach and the parents, and also between the player and parents with several real-life examples. We also saw, in this sense, the importance of focusing on competencies, that is, on defining what the expected behavior standards are, both for players and for parents and coaches.

It is important to be self-critical and evaluate ourselves in each of these competencies because, without a doubt, we have aspects to improve.

10.1 Guidelines For Youth Sport Organizations

We must encourage youth sports organizations to promote the learning of these competencies and values that are key for sports and that which also bring more harmony in playing sports.

I strongly believe that youth sports organizations have a tremendous opportunity to strengthen their value proposition toward children and teenagers. Many players spend years in the same YSO practicing the same sport. The amount of time that the players spend in practice and the number of interactions between them is very high. Given this, I think it is an excellent opportunity to train coaches, parents, and specially the kids in these competencies, soft skills, and values that will allow kids to build those capacities for their adult life.

Is competency-based training sufficient? I think is not enough. I believe that it is just the beginning of something. And it is important to bring to light the essence of sports and create awareness of the opportunity that sports gives us to change our behaviors and to be better human beings.

10.2   Guidelines For Coaches

No matter how comprehensive the competencies are, the coach must always connect with what the player wants at that moment. The coach should know and define (or at least just perceive) what it is that fulfills the player, what is better for his development and personal growth.

Coaches should teach the athletes to focus more on "the journey" rather than on the outcomes. During the journey, the youth athletes will maximize their potential and their learning experience.

Coaches are key influencers of children, and they can cause significant changes in their lives. By using the youth sport competency model as part of their training development programs, they can create new incentives in children and young players, as well as ownership of their progress.

10.3   Guidelines For Parents

Players, supported by their parents, must choose what are the key competences they want to develop first. Every player is different and unique. It is not possible to develop all the skills, so players need to understand what makes them most happy and fulfilled at each moment. The main goal is for the player to experience a sustained state of inner joy.

Parents should support their kids without judging, just telling them they love watching them playing. It's all the kids need. As a parent, enjoy the experience of looking at your child playing sports. You have this unique opportunity every season. Share this feeling with your child.

Take time to select the YSO, review the development programs, and see how they achieve this. Choose the right coach. Then let the coach do his work.

Teach your children to focus on what they have instead of focusing on what is missing. The key to achieving this is through gratitude. Teach them to be grateful for everything they have achieved and not focus on everything that is missing. Enjoy the journey. There are many things to be grateful for.

Be grateful as parents. Be grateful for having a son in good health playing sports; be grateful for your kids having the opportunity to have new friends, to be part of a team, interacting with teammates and with the coach. Just be grateful.

RISK-TAKING:
"The things you regret most in life are the risks you didn't take."

ATTENTION TO DETAILS:
"It is the little details that are vital. Little
things make big things happen."

11

K12STARS INITIATIVE

In July 2015, I was on vacations with my family in Argentina, and we visited a very small town in the interior. My children wanted to practice soccer, and we went to a local club to train. I had a conversation with the coaches, and they told me about an initiative that filled the boys with joy.

It was about a sticker album of the club itself, including the teams and individual stickers of each of the players. Imagine these kids, between eight and fourteen years old, collecting stickers of themselves, having their name and position on it. Traditionally, these children collect sticker albums of famous players or events, like the Soccer World Cup, where there are hundreds of star professional players from all over the world.

After that experience, I was wondering myself for a couple of months:

- How can we give young athletes back all their effort and dedication to the sports they love?
- How can we release some pressure on them?
- How can we educate them with soft skills through sports?
- How can we give them more joy in a friendly gaming environment?
- How can we let them feel like a professional sport star?

And that's when K12Stars comes in. From K12Stars's perspective, kids are the stars. Collecting a sticker album of themselves provides an inner sensation of "feeling like a professional player." What a nice feeling, right? How sport can help them feel more joy.

Since then I did not stop working on designing several value propositions for clubs. Through different games, like the sticker albums and others, clubs will be able to raise funds to support and improve their training programs.

These games, for example, also include the learning of values and competences where parents, coaches, and players can be trained in these aspects that are so important for the future of young players, even outside of sport.

The idea was so innovative that in 2019 we filed a provisional patent application within the USPTO office in the United States. In 2020, we filed a non-provisional patent application and K12Stars become a "Patent Pending" status company.

The title of this book, *The Star Is Inside*, is a summary that describes how the truly star is the child and the full potential is inside himself.

I am convinced that initiatives like this promote the healthy growth of the entire community to a next level of consciousness, including parents, coaches, and players.

12

CLOSING MESSAGE

As I said at the beginning of the book, many children quit sports because they are not enjoying the experience.

We must return to the essence of sport. Back to basics. Sports is recreation. It is about joining, staying together, making friends, working with a team, exerting effort, but above everything else, sports is joy. It is not about "us versus them" as I stated in previous chapter regarding the definition of the new paradigm of success.

Sports give us a unique opportunity to educate our children beyond the beliefs we have received when we were children, no matter the role we play, as a parent or as a coach. It is the opportunity that sport gives them to grow up healthy, to make new friends, to cultivate values, and to be aware of the correct behaviors for their adult life.

I hope that we can work together with sports organizations to promote this new culture of teaching sports with values and skills based on expected behaviors. In short, this new approach to work, coordinated between parents and coaches, ends up leaving enormous benefits for those whom we love the most: our children.

In this sense, I will continue identifying growth opportunities for our kids because I believe behaviors are a consequence of something, we have inside ourselves. Behaviors are part of our beliefs, our mental programming. This mental programming and beliefs need to be changed or rewired so new behaviors are sustainable.

Maybe this is going to be my new research for the next book.

APPENDIX

SUMMARY OF COMPETENCES
FOR PLAYERS

This section is intended to be a guide for parents and coaches to work with players and help them develop these skills. For each of them, I have selected a "famous quote" related to this competency, then the competency definition, its expected behaviors, real examples in the world of youth sports, and a very simple quiz to make them think about real-life situations where these competencies and behaviors can be applied.

- Quote: "Dedication and commitment are what transforms dreams into realities."

- What is commitment?
  - o Commitment is the attitude of sincere and dedicated focus on purpose. Having commitment suggests that they have the heart and motivation to push through the tough times.

- Expected behaviors:
  - o Having a detailed plan on how to achieve goals
  - o Focusing on the process more than results
  - o Being a student of your sport
  - o Staying positive and motivated when struggling; focusing on the solution, not the problem

- Examples in youth sports:
  - o Desiring to achieve success
  - o Working hard to achieve your goals
  - o Not missing any practice; staying tuned and focusing on practice.

- Quiz:
  - o What is an example of dedication and commitment in sports?
    - Getting up 6:00 a.m. on Sunday to play a game in another city an hour away from home
    - Attending all practices and staying focused at all times
    - Striving to improve technical skills and fitness
    - All of the above

- Quote: "Without self-discipline, success is impossible, period."

- What is discipline?
  - o It is the ability of an individual to control oneself and behave in a manner that is compliant with the rules of the sport. Discipline will teach players that it's important to choose what's best for the long-term instead of seeking instant gratification.

- Expected behaviors:
  - o Sacrificing some things
  - o Dealing with losses to improve performance next time
  - o Setting and accomplishing goals

- Examples in youth sports:
  - o Being ready on time to get to practice on time
  - o Following the coach's instructions during practice
  - o Maintaining a good diet and having a good daily rest time

- Quiz:
  - o Which of these expected behaviors do not help improve your sports discipline?
    - I sleep very late the night before a very early game.
    - I eat a lot of food shortly before a game.
    - I am not following the coach's instructions during practice.
    - All of the above

- Quote: "Integrity is doing the right thing, even when no one is watching."

- What is integrity?
  - o Integrity concerns the moral or ethical aspect of sports. Having integrity means you are true to yourself and would do nothing that demeans or dishonors you.

- Expected behaviors:
  - o Keeping your promises even if it takes extra effort
  - o Not gossiping or talking badly about someone
  - o Not letting someone else take the blame for something you did

- Examples in youth sports:
  - o Accepting your role on the team, but keep working hard so your role can increase
  - o Not talking about your teammates or coaches behind their back
  - o Keeping your word. Your word is "true." Do what you say you are going to do every time.

- Quiz:
  - o Which of these actions demonstrate integrity?
    - Stepping over a piece of trash on the field, then deciding to go back and picking it up
    - Intentionally causing injury to another because you can get away with it
    - Not shaking hands with your opponent after a game

- Quote: "Respect should be the first thing you give."

- What is respect?
  - o Respect is having a regard for other people and their lives; it is showing those around us compassion and empathy.

- Expected behaviors:
  - o Respecting your opponent: There is no place for harassing comments or other actions that might humiliate the other side.
  - o Respecting the officials: If there's a questionable call during a game, athletes should quietly and appropriately ask for an explanation.
  - o Respecting the game: Anything that is not about playing the game or communicating with teammates can lead to disrespect for the sport.

- Examples in youth sports:
  - o Honoring the game, accepting penalties when you break the rules
  - o Cheering for your team in a positive, encouraging way
  - o Letting your play speak for itself; no fighting words, insults, or threats

- Quiz:
  - o The opponent stumbles and falls to the floor in pain. Which of these expected behaviors show respect for the opponent?
    - You laugh at the fall and look for the laughter of your players.
    - You ask your opponent if he's okay, and you help him stand up.
    - You complain about your opponent's attitude.

- Quote: "Teamwork divides the tasks and multiplies the success."

- What is teamwork?
  - o Teamwork can be defined as individuals working together to achieve a common goal.

- Expected behaviors:
  - o Supporting group decisions, even if not in total agreement
  - o Sharing credit for good ideas or accomplishments with peers, team members, and others
  - o Cooperatively working with peers, team members, and others to set responsibilities

- Examples in youth sports:
  - o Being open to a suggestion from other player or from your coach
  - o Winning or loosing together with the team
  - o Trusting and relying on each of the team members

- Quiz:
  - o You are the team captain, and the coach has defined the game strategy for today. The game starts, and things are not going as planned. What do you do?
    - Be patient and persistent, reinforcing the strategy to the team and continue following the game plan.
    - Change the strategy and directions to your teammates.
    - Start complaining about the situation, influencing the team behavior negatively.

- Quote: "Accountability: The glue that ties commitment to results."

- What is accountability?
  - o Accountability is taking or being assigned responsibility for something that you have done or something you are supposed to do.

- Expected behaviors:
  - o Showing up to work on time and following instructions
  - o Staying focused on tasks despite distractions and interruptions
  - o Not making excuses for errors or problems, acknowledging and correcting mistakes.

- Examples in youth sports:
  - o Asking to be held accountable for the commitments it takes to achieve your goals
  - o Giving thanks to your coach who never lets you give less than your best
  - o Being patient and embracing the struggle
  - o Not making up excuses if you lose; not rubbing it in if you win

- Quiz:
  - o During the game today, you know you are not performing well, not doing what you should do in your position. How do you show accountability and take ownership of the situation?
    - You start complaining about other teammates' mistakes.
    - You focus on your role and start paying attention on what to do in your position.
    - You ask the coach to be replace it because you feel frustrated.

- Quote: "Don't wait for the perfect moment. Take the moment and make it perfect."

- What is initiative?
  - Initiative is all about taking charge. An initiative is the first in a series of actions. Initiative also means a personal quality that shows a willingness to get things done.

- Expected behaviors:
  - Volunteering to help peers when one's workload is light
  - Suggesting ways to solve problems, etc., without being asked
  - Being a "self-starter," not waiting to be assigned something

- Examples in youth sports:
  - Proactively asking your coach for feedback or things to improve your performance
  - Inviting your teammates to have an extra practice
  - Reminding your teammates to pay attention during practice
  - Making yourself available to help your coach with the equipment

- Quiz:
  - You met all the players an hour before the game, but the coach has not arrived. The team has been waiting for more than fifteen minutes. How do you show initiative?
    - You get away from your team and start stretching alone.
    - You ask your team to start doing the warm-up all together.
    - You continue talking to other players until the coach arrives.

- Quote: "Every accomplishment began with a decision to try."

- What is decision-making?
  - o Decision-making is the cognitive operation of selecting a response from a range of available responses in circumstances where an action is needed.

- Expected behaviors:
  - o Quickly making decisions during tough situations
  - o Independently making decisions
  - o Anticipating the consequences of decisions

- Examples in youth sports:
  - o Studying the opponents' patterns. This understanding can narrow the number of choices and responses to their moves.
  - o Identifying cues. Responding to cues narrows the choice of responses and speeds up decision-making.
  - o Practicing responding to different competitive conditions
  - o Anticipating opponents' actions

- Quiz:
  - o Which of these components are important in order to make a decision during a game?
    - Thinking about similar field of play situations during this game or previous games
    - Analyzing alternatives and quickly deciding the option of play
    - Anticipating the expected outcome, being one step ahead of the game
    - All of the above

- Quote: "When we are no longer able to change a situation, we are challenged to change ourselves."

- What is adaptability?
  - o Adaptability is the quality of being able to adjust to new conditions. It is the ability to learn from experience and change to become more effective.

- Expected behaviors:
  - o Focusing on the beneficial aspects of change
  - o Quickly modifying one's behavior to deal with changes in the environment
  - o Not persisting with ineffective behaviors

- Examples in youth sports:
  - o Learning to play new positions in the field
  - o Playing different competitions
  - o Following change directions suggested by the coach

- Quiz:
  - o We reached the final of the tournament, but we have four injured players who will not be able to play the final. The coach asks me that in this match, I will not be a forward, but I will have to play defense. My parents are upset because I have always played as a forward. What should I do?
    - Adapt to the coach's request and remember when I played defense to give my best in this final
    - Ask my parents to speak to the coach to change my position before the final
    - Start the final playing defense and as soon as I can go to play forward

- Quote: "The greatest weapon against stress is our ability to choose one thought over another."

- What is stress management?
  - o Stress management refers to the environmental, physiological, cognitive, and behavioral techniques employed by an individual to manage the factors and components that underlie the stress, such as anxiety, nervousness, apprehension, or worry.

- Expected behaviors:
  - o Handling a heavy workload
  - o Handling distractions or interruptions to work
  - o Dealing with rush situations
  - o Remaining flexible, open, and decisive in the face of changing needs

- Examples in youth sports
  - o Breathing deeply
  - o Applying muscle relaxation techniques (such as progressive, self-directed types)
  - o Visualizing positive images (both internal and external).

- Quiz:
  - o It's time to go to sleep since tomorrow I have a very important game early in the morning. I have normal nerves before an important game. What can I do to relax and have a good rest?
    - Take a few deep breaths, imagining good times during tomorrow's game
    - Seek to sleep with a positive attitude, trusting that I will give my best performance
    - Think that tomorrow I will be even more nervous than today, and I don't know what will happen
    - The first two options

- Quote: "A lot of problems in sports disappear if we talk to each other, instead of about each other."

- What is problem-solving?
  - o Problem-solving involves goal-directed thinking and action in situations for which no routine solutions exist.

- Expected behaviors:
  - o Accurately assessing the situation and reaching a positive solution
  - o Helping improve team chemistry
  - o Learning ways to balance schedules between school and sports

- Examples in youth sports:
  - o Finding alternative solutions rather than panicking or getting blocked
  - o Fixing performance slumps
  - o Dealing with playing time issues

- Quiz:
  - o The team is not playing well. We have lost the last four games in a row. What can I do to help solve the problem?
    - Have a positive attitude, connect the experience with my personal goals and learning objectives, identify potential improvements
    - Talk about the low performance of some players
    - Complain about the coach and the game strategy used

- Quote: "The only place that success comes before work is in the dictionary."

- What is persistence?
  - o Persistence is the attitude or behavior of someone who continues to do or try to do something in a determined way.

- Expected behaviors:
  - o Working to achieve a goal despite barriers or difficulties
  - o Working to overcome obstacles by changing strategies, doubling efforts, using multiple approaches, etc.
  - o Adjusting focus when it becomes evident that a goal cannot be achievable

- Examples in youth sports:
  - o Overcoming mistakes and setbacks
  - o Adapting to change
  - o Focusing on goals daily

- Quiz:
  - o I have been practicing this sport for three years, and I am unable to rise to the next level of competition. What I can do?
    - Quit this sport and look for other options
    - Complain to the club because it is an injustice that they do not raise me to the next team
    - Understand what I have to improve and continue working hard to get to the next level

- Quote: "The things you regret most in life are the risks you didn't take."

- What is risk-taking?
  - o Risk-taking means getting out of your comfort zone, pushing your limits, and doing things on the field of play that may lead to greater success.

- Expected behaviors:
  - o Making decisions when the probability of success is unclear
  - o Making decisions that involve risk
  - o Trying new but unproven approaches to solving problems
  - o Balancing risks to take to avoid sport injuries

- Examples in youth sports:
  - o Participating in try-outs for the middle school and high school teams
  - o Practicing different alternatives to resolve a tactic situation
  - o Focusing on the game to identify opportunities to make a difference

- Quiz:
  - o We are winning the match by one-point difference, and there are only two minutes left to finish. Our fans yell, "Come on, guys, pressure, fight, play hard, play aggressive." In this environment, excited by the climate of the fans, I am going to play a ball beyond the limit of my body, putting my physical integrity and that of my opponent at risk. Is it a correct decision?
    - ▪ Yes, because the fans are asking for sacrifice and the team must play aggressive to win.
    - ▪ No, because I am taking too much risk and I can suffer an injury, leaving my team with one less player.
    - ▪ Yes, because I must cut the game to save time so the game is over.

- Quote: "It is the little details that are vital. Little things make big things happen."

- What is attention to details?
  - o It achieves thoroughness and accuracy when accomplishing a task through concern for all the areas involved.

- Expected behaviors:
  - o Accurately and carefully following established procedures for completing work tasks
  - o Ensuring that all details of a task are accomplishable
  - o Keeping track of many small details without forgetting any
  - o Keeping concentration over a while

- Examples in youth sports:
  - o Creating a routine or predefine steps before the game to gain concentration and staying focused on the game
  - o Paying attention and following the instructions of your coach regarding technical details
  - o Avoiding multitasking activities, focusing your attention in one activity at a time

- Quiz:
  - o Today is game day. Which of these attitudes allow you to pay attention to detail and focus on the game?
    - Have breakfast, think about the game, visualize myself having a good performance
    - Have breakfast while playing on my cell phone and chatting with my friends at the same time
    - During the match, pay attention to the screams of the rival fans

- Quote: "You never learn anything talking. You learn when you ask and when you practice."

- What is applied learning?
  - o Applied learning refers to an educational approach whereby students learn by engaging in direct application of skills, theories, and models.

- Expected behaviors:
  - o Actively participating in learning activities
  - o Promptly assimilating and applying coach-related information
  - o Readily absorbing and comprehending new information from formal and informal learning experiences
  - o Putting new knowledge, understanding, or skill to practical use

- Examples in youth sports:
  - o Knowing and understanding the technical instructions of the coach
  - o Practicing the technique of movements
  - o Achieving automatic technical movements during competitions

- Quiz:
  - o Did you understand what applied learning means?
    - Applied learning is the verbal stage, where you are a theoretical expert in the sport you practice, technically knowing the physical movements of your body
    - Applied learning is the motor stage, where you put into practice the theoretical knowledge that your coach explains to you
    - Applied learning is the automatic stage, where after a long time of practice, the technical movements are carried out automatically
    - All of the above

- Quote: "Believe in this: The future can be better than the present, and I have the power to make it so."

- What is self-motivation?
  - o Self-motivation is, in its simplest form, the force that drives you to do things. It drives people to keep going even in the face of setbacks, to take up opportunities and to show commitment to what they want to achieve.

- Expected behaviors:
  - o Looking on the bright side, thinking positively
  - o Showing ability to "bounce back" after a setback, keeping positivity in the face of challenges
  - o Keeping a growth mindset, improving skills through hard work and effort

- Examples in youth sports:
  - o Loving to play the sport, having passion about it
  - o Focusing on what excites you about playing and performing
  - o Leaving 100 percent of your effort during training
  - o Celebrating the good times

- Quiz:
  - o Which of these types of motivation come from within yourself?
    - Play the final and hope to win the long-awaited trophy
    - Share a breakfast with the team at the hotel before a game
    - The desire within a player to improve, achieve, and succeed

- Quote: "We are stronger when we listen and smarter when we share."

- What is communication?
  - o Communication is the process of giving a message containing information and understanding from one person to another. In simple words, it is a process of transmitting and sharing ideas, opinions, facts, values etc. from one person to another.

- Expected behaviors:
  - o Providing positive messages
  - o Receiving instructions, orders, or assignments
  - o Clearly communicating ideas in a group setting
  - o Listening and being receptive to others' ideas or suggestions

- Examples in youth sports:
  - o Talking to your teammates during the game
  - o Asking your coach for feedback
  - o Communicating your concerns to the coach, being proactive

- Quiz:
  - o I was playing forward position the whole season, and today I was on the bench and only played fifteen minutes in defense position. I'm really upset. What can I do?
    - Ask your parents' help so they can talk to the coach
    - Talk to the coach in the next practice and ask him about the reason for this change
    - Complain with your teammates and ask them for a reason of this change

- Quote: "The most powerful leadership tool you have is your own personal example."

- What is leadership?
  o Leadership is the art of motivating a group of people to act toward achieving a common goal.

- Expected behaviors:
  o Building relationships with your teammates, peers, and players
  o Seeing the positive side of passion
  o Motivating other players to be better every day

- Examples in youth sports:
  o Being a role model
  o Being a team captain or following your team captain's instructions
  o Remaining decisive and confident, making decisions, and communicating to others

- Quiz:
  o It is the final of the championship, and the game has just started. I am the captain, and the team is not playing well. The other team converts since we made a silly mistake in defense. The team is demotivated, surprised by the mistake made. What should I do as captain to show leadership?
    - Complain to the player who made the mistake
    - Motivate the team, order the game, speak positively, encourage the players to seek to reverse the result and win the game
    - Complain to the coach about the player who made the mistake